ATLANTIC
ANIMALS
AT RISK

ATLANTIC
PUFFINS

MEGAN BORGERT-SPANIOL

Checkerboard
Library

An Imprint of Abdo Publishing
abdobooks.com

▶ ABDOBOOKS.COM

Published by Abdo Publishing, a division of ABDO, PO Box 398166, Minneapolis, Minnesota 55439.
Copyright © 2019 by Abdo Consulting Group, Inc. International copyrights reserved in all countries.
No part of this book may be reproduced in any form without written permission from the publisher.
Checkerboard Library™ is a trademark and logo of Abdo Publishing.

Printed in the United States of America, North Mankato, Minnesota
102018
012019

 THIS BOOK CONTAINS
RECYCLED MATERIALS

Design and Production: Mighty Media, Inc.
Editor: Liz Salzmann
Cover Photographs: Shutterstock
Interior Photographs: Alamy, p. 25; Brett Albanese/Georgia DNR/Flickr, p. 19; iStockphoto, pp. 9, 11, 12–13, 15, 23, 26, 29; Shutterstock, pp. 5, 7, 16–17, 20, 28

Library of Congress Control Number: 2018948504

Publisher's Cataloging-in-Publication Data
Names: Borgert-Spaniol, Megan, author.
Title: Atlantic puffins / by Megan Borgert-Spaniol.
Description: Minneapolis, Minnesota : Abdo Publishing, 2019 | Series: Arctic animals at risk | Includes online resources and index.
Identifiers: ISBN 9781532116957 (lib. bdg.) | ISBN 9781532159794 (ebook)
Subjects: LCSH: Atlantic puffin--Juvenile literature. | Birds--Behavior--Arctic regions--Juvenile literature. | Environmental protection--Arctic regions--Juvenile literature. | Habitat protection--Juvenile literature.
Classification: DDC 598.33--dc23

Stark County District Library
www.StarkLibrary.org
330.452.0665

MAY - - 2019

TABLE OF
CONTENTS

▷ CHAPTER 1
COLORFUL COLONIES — **4**

▷ CHAPTER 2
ATLANTIC PUFFINS AT RISK — **6**

▷ CHAPTER 3
NORTHERN SEA SWIMMERS — **8**

▷ CHAPTER 4
COURTING AND NESTING — **10**

▷ CHAPTER 5
CHICKS TO FLEDGLINGS — **14**

▷ CHAPTER 6
DISAPPEARING FISH — **18**

▷ CHAPTER 7
A CONCERNING FUTURE — **22**

▷ CHAPTER 8
SAVING ATLANTIC PUFFINS — **24**

ATLANTIC PUFFIN FACT SHEET — **28**

WHAT CAN YOU DO? — **29**

GLOSSARY — **30**

ONLINE RESOURCES — **31**

INDEX — **32**

COLORFUL COLONIES

O ff the southern coast of Iceland, the Westman Islands rise up from the Atlantic Ocean. The islands' grassy slopes lead to cliffs that plunge into the blue sea. For part of the year, these cliffs host the islands' colorful bird **inhabitants**, Atlantic puffins.

The Westman Islands are home to one of the world's largest Atlantic puffin nesting colonies. During breeding season, thousands of puffin pairs dot the islands in black, white, and orange. The sight draws many admiring human visitors. The birds are beloved for their upright waddle and bright, triangular bills.

Several birds take flight toward the sea and return with fish for their chicks. Soon the chicks will grow strong enough to leave the nest. Then, the members of the colony will scatter. The birds will leave their nests and return to the open sea.

Atlantic puffins are the smallest puffin species. ▶

ATLANTIC PUFFINS AT RISK

Atlantic puffins are members of the Alcidae family of seabirds. They live mainly in the North Atlantic Ocean. But in some regions their range extends to the southern Arctic Ocean. During breeding season, the puffins nest on coastlines throughout their range.

When seen in large breeding colonies, Atlantic puffins appear to be plentiful. But the sight can be deceiving. The Westman Islands colony is one of many that are showing signs of distress. Atlantic puffins' food source is threatened by human activities, such as overfishing. The birds are also at risk because of climate change.

WHAT IS CLIMATE CHANGE?

Climate change is periodic change in Earth's weather patterns. In recent years, scientists have observed an increase in the rate of climate change. Most scientists agree this is due to humans burning **fossil fuels**. Burning fossil fuels produces **greenhouse gases** which trap heat in Earth's atmosphere. This has led to rising global temperatures.

In recent years, researchers have found that many puffins, especially chicks, are not getting enough food. These young puffins don't live long enough to breed. Because of this and other threats, many puffin populations are declining.

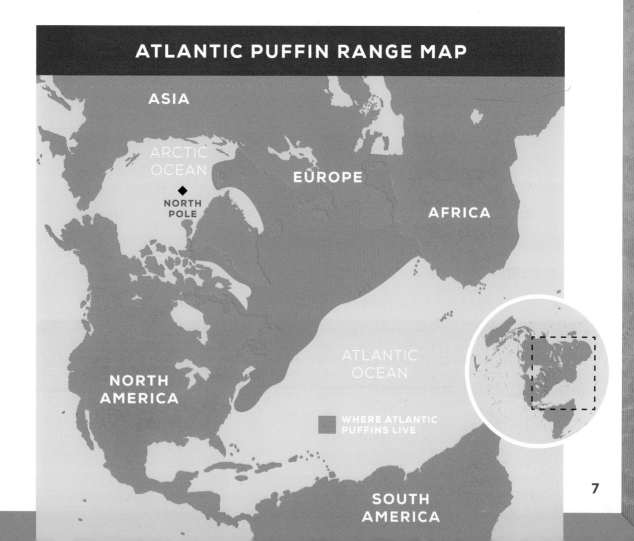

ATLANTIC PUFFIN RANGE MAP

ASIA

ARCTIC OCEAN

EUROPE

NORTH POLE

AFRICA

NORTH AMERICA

ATLANTIC OCEAN

WHERE ATLANTIC PUFFINS LIVE

SOUTH AMERICA

NORTHERN SEA SWIMMERS

Atlantic puffins are well-known for their colorful coastal colonies. But the birds spend most of their lives far offshore. For about eight months a year, the seabirds float in the open sea.

The puffins are well adapted to cold ocean waters. **Waterproof** feathers protect their bodies from the icy water. This keeps the birds warm as they float on the surface and swim underwater.

Atlantic puffins are also built to **forage** at sea. They feed on small fish, such as herring, capelin, and sand eels. Atlantic puffins dive underwater to reach this prey. Their dives usually last about 20 to 30 seconds. However, a puffin can hold its breath for up to a minute.

Compact bodies and strong wings allow Atlantic puffins to dive up to 200 feet (60 m) deep. The birds steer with their **webbed** feet and flap their wings to move forward. They look as though they are flying underwater!

Besides eating fish, Atlantic puffins also eat crustaceans and mollusks and drink seawater.

As they dive, Atlantic puffins scoop up as many fish as will fit in their bills. These birds collect an average of ten fish per dive. However, they can hold much more. Specialized bills allow Atlantic puffins to hold more than 50 fish at once. Spines inside the birds' bills keep the fish in place, even as the puffins open their mouths for more.

COURTING AND NESTING

Atlantic puffins thrive at sea. But they have an important reason to fly back to land once a year. It is on Northern Atlantic coastlines where the puffins breed each spring.

Most puffins do not breed until they are five years old. At that time, they often return to the colony where they hatched. Scientists are not sure how puffins find their way back to their birthplaces. Experts think the birds may create mental maps of their home colonies using sounds, smells, and visual cues.

As breeding season arrives, puffins begin to change in appearance. Their faces turn from gray to white. Their feet and bills, which are dull gray during winter, take on bright colors. Scientists think these bright colors may help puffins attract mates.

Once Atlantic puffins pair up, they may perform courtship displays. Pairs often rub or tap their bills together to show affection. This behavior is known as billing.

Atlantic puffins' bills grow larger as they age. Scientists think bill size may be a sign of experience and maturity to puffins looking for a mate.

Atlantic puffins usually reunite with the same mate every breeding season. Often, the puffins will even return to the same nesting site. Atlantic puffins nest along steep, rocky cliffs overlooking the sea. These sites provide easy access to fish in coastal waters. They also provide many sheltered spaces between large rocks.

Atlantic puffins build nests in these spaces. Or, they nest in burrows they dig in the soil. Inside a burrow or rocky crevice, Atlantic puffins build soft nests of grasses and feathers.

A female puffin lays a single egg in her nest. She and her mate take turns incubating the egg. They keep the egg warm against a patch of featherless skin on their undersides. This is called a brood patch. It allows the birds' body heat to transfer to the egg. After about six weeks of incubation, the egg hatches.

 Puffins make nests out of grasses, sticks, and feathers.

13

CHICKS TO FLEDGLINGS

Puffin chicks are also known as pufflings. When they hatch, the chicks appear very different from their colorful parents. Pufflings have black feet and bills. They are also covered in black feathers. This thick covering of soft down feathers keeps the chicks warm.

Pufflings remain inside their nests after they hatch. They rely on their parents to feed them. Every day, adult puffins fly out to sea to find food for their chicks. They return to land with bills full of fish.

During these flights to and from land, Atlantic puffins look out for danger. Their main predators are great black-backed gulls. These birds can attack puffins in mid-flight. Herring gulls are also predators. They will eat puffin eggs and chicks. Herring gulls have been known to steal fish right out of puffins' bills!

Atlantic puffins can fly 55 miles per hour (88 kmh). As they fly, they flap their wings up to 400 times per minute!

Back at their nests, puffins feed their catches to their chicks. They often do so by dropping the fish on the nest floor for the chicks to pick up. This feeding **routine** occurs several times a day until the chicks gain enough weight to **fledge**. This normally takes about six weeks. However, chicks take longer to fledge when fish are scarce.

When chicks are strong enough to fly, they leave their nests. Fledglings fly away from their colony toward the open sea. Fully independent, they must protect themselves from predators, storms, and other threats. They learn where to feed and how to find a mate. Young Atlantic puffins remain at sea for several years until they reach breeding age. Only then will the birds return to land to raise chicks, often at the same sites where they hatched.

Puffins' burrows can have multiple entrances or branch out to multiple nests.

CHAPTER 6

DISAPPEARING FISH

Atlantic puffins' yearly visits to breeding colonies make it possible for researchers to study the birds. Over the past 25 years, scientists have gathered data from various breeding colonies in North America and Europe. In recent years, they have discovered an alarming trend. Many Atlantic puffins are starving.

Scientists have linked this trend to the effects of climate change. As global temperatures rise, North Atlantic waters are warming. This affects fish that are adapted to cold water. In response, these fish populations shift further north to colder **habitats**. This affects animals that eat the fish, including Atlantic puffins.

Puffin chicks are especially **vulnerable** to these changes in ocean temperature. They rely on a diet of small fish, such as sand eels. But these fish need to live in cold waters. As the ocean warms, these fish populations are becoming less abundant. So, puffin parents are bringing their chicks other types of fish instead.

One new type of fish is the butterfish. It is commonly found in more southern waters. Its recent presence in northern waters is likely due to warming temperatures. But puffin chicks cannot eat butterfish. In 2012, researchers documented a chick in a nesting colony off the coast of Maine. The chick was surrounded by butterfish that its parents had caught. But the fish were too large for the chick to swallow. Because of this, the chick starved to death.

Butterfish are much rounder than herring, sand eels, and other fish that puffins eat.

Scientists believe there could be hundreds of dead Atlantic puffins for each one found washed ashore.

Scientists have observed chick starvation in colonies across the puffins' range. They have also observed dead puffins washed ashore on both sides of the Atlantic. Many of these puffins also showed signs of starvation.

Climate change is affecting Atlantic puffins across the North Atlantic. But other human activities also threaten the birds. These activities include overfishing.

Overfishing further reduces the number of fish **available** to Atlantic puffins. For example, huge numbers of Atlantic herring are caught for lobster bait in Maine. These fish are important to the lobster industry. But they are also a key part of the Atlantic puffin's diet. Herring overfishing has also been blamed for reducing puffin food sources in Norway.

Another human activity that threatens Atlantic puffins is offshore oil development. Drilling and shipping oil in the ocean can lead to oil spills. Oil can damage the puffins' **waterproof** feathers, which keep the birds warm. The puffins also become sick if they swallow oil while cleaning it off their feathers. A major oil spill near a breeding colony could wipe out thousands of puffins.

A CONCERNING FUTURE

Overfishing and oil spills threaten Atlantic puffin populations across their range. But the greatest threat to the future of the species is climate change. This is because global warming comes with many effects. Scientists don't know if or how Atlantic puffins will adapt to these effects.

Along with shifting fish populations, another effect of climate change is rising sea levels. Scientists worry that this could flood puffin breeding islands. Climate change also causes more extreme weather. Atlantic puffins may not be able to survive severe storms, especially if they are underweight from lack of food.

Based on recent trends, researchers **predict** future **declines** in Atlantic puffin populations. Experts believe the population in Europe will decline by up to 79 percent by 2065. The majority of the species are in this population. Because of this, such declines would greatly affect the global population of Atlantic puffins.

Rising sea levels can make it harder for puffins to find places to build nests.

SAVING ATLANTIC PUFFINS

Because of human activity, the future is uncertain for Atlantic puffins. This is why conservationists argue it is humans' responsibility to protect the birds. One of the first steps in protecting a species is the official recognition of its threatened status.

In 2015, the International Union for the Conservation of Nature (IUCN) listed the Atlantic puffin as **Vulnerable**. This status means the species is considered to be facing a high risk of extinction in the wild. The IUCN recommends that certain actions be taken to help protect Atlantic puffins. But it is up to individual countries to carry out these actions.

IUCN

The International Union for the Conservation of Nature is a global authority on the status of wildlife. It collects scientific data and experts' studies to determine the status of a species. Then, governments and conservation organizations use this information to make decisions about species protection.

Several nations in the Atlantic puffin's range have already taken steps to protect the birds. For example, Iceland has a long history of hunting the seabirds. But in 2016, local authorities limited this hunting season to three days. Norway, Scotland, and other North Atlantic nations have banned puffin hunting altogether.

People use nets to catch Atlantic puffins.

Tree mallow is a flowering plant that has overtaken puffin habitats on the Scottish island of Craigleith. The organization SOS Puffin helps puffins by cutting down tree mallow.

West of the Atlantic, the United States has taken steps to protect the puffins' habitat. In 2016, the nation recognized the first marine national monument in the Atlantic Ocean. The Northeast Canyons and Seamounts Marine National Monument (NCSMNM) is about 150 miles off the coast of Cape Cod, Massachusetts.

NCSMNM covers nearly 5,000 square miles (13,000 sq km). It includes the offshore habitat where many Atlantic puffins live during winter. As a national monument, this habitat is protected against future industrial activities, including commercial fishing.

Protecting Atlantic puffin habitats from commercial fishing is an important step in saving the species. However, experts argue that climate change must also be addressed. This means limiting emissions of greenhouse gases, which cause global warming.

These are not easy tasks. Many regions rely on commercial fishing to bring in money. And many nations get their energy from burning fossil fuels. So, lawmakers often disagree on how to limit these industrial activities.

Meanwhile, conservation organizations are keeping a close watch on Atlantic puffins. One organization is the National Audubon Society's Project Puffin. This program is tracking puffin diets, foraging habits, and survival rates. This data will shed light on how climate change and commercial fishing are affecting the species over time. It may also provide answers for how to ensure a healthy future for Atlantic puffins.

ATLANTIC PUFFIN
FACT SHEET

SCIENTIFIC NAME: *Fratercula arctica*

LENGTH: 10 inches (25 cm)

WEIGHT: 17.5 ounces (500 g)

DIET: carnivore

AVERAGE LIFESPAN IN THE WILD: 20 or more years

IUCN STATUS: Vulnerable

WHAT CAN
YOU DO?

You can take action to help Atlantic puffins and other Arctic animals at risk!

▷ Give money to or volunteer for Atlantic puffin conservation organizations, such as the National Audubon Society. You can even adopt an Atlantic puffin through Audubon's Project Puffin!

▷ Write to local lawmakers asking them to support policies that protect Atlantic puffins. These policies include laws that limit **greenhouse gas** emissions.

▷ Tell your friends and family about climate change and how it affects Arctic wildlife such as Atlantic puffins.

▷ Reduce your individual use of **fossil fuels** by choosing to bike, walk, or take the bus instead of riding in a car.

GLOSSARY

available—able to be had or used.

crevice—a narrow opening due to a split or a crack in something.

decline—to become lower in amount.

document—to create a record of something through research and observation.

ensure—to make sure, certain, or safe.

fledge—to develop the feathers necessary for flying. A young bird that has gained its feathers and can leave the nest is called a fledgling.

forage—to search.

fossil fuel—a fuel formed in the earth from the remains of plants or animals. Coal, oil, and natural gas are fossil fuels.

greenhouse gas—a gas, such as carbon dioxide, that traps heat in Earth's atmosphere.

habitat—a place where a living thing is naturally found.

incubate—to keep eggs warm, often by sitting on them, so they will hatch.

inhabitant—a person or animal that lives in a particular place.

predict—to guess something ahead of time on the basis of observation, experience, or reasoning.

routine—a regular order of actions or way of doing something.

status—a state or a condition.

thrive—to do well.

vulnerable—able to be hurt or attacked. An animal has a vulnerable status when it is likely to become endangered.

waterproof—not allowing water to pass through.

webbed—having skin connecting the fingers or toes.

ONLINE
RESOURCES

Booklinks
NONFICTION NETWORK
FREE! ONLINE NONFICTION RESOURCES

To learn more about Atlantic puffins, visit abdobooklinks.com. **These links are routinely monitored and updated to provide the most current information available.**

INDEX

B
babies, 4, 7, 14, 16, 18, 19, 21
bills, 4, 9, 10, 14
breeding, 4, 6, 7, 10, 13, 16, 18, 21, 22
butterfish, 18, 19

C
climate change, 6, 18, 21, 22, 27
coastal colonies, 4, 6, 8, 10, 13, 19, 26
commercial fishing, 6, 21, 27
conservation efforts, 24, 25, 26, 27

D
diet, 8, 9, 14, 18, 19, 21, 27
diving, 8, 9

E
eggs, 13, 14
Europe, 18, 22

F
feathers, 8, 13, 14, 21
flying, 4, 8, 10, 14, 16
foraging, 8, 27

H
habitat, 6, 18, 22, 26, 27
herring, 8, 14, 21
humans, 4, 6, 21, 24, 27
hunting, 8, 9

I
Iceland, 4, 25
International Union for the Conservation of Nature, 24

N
nesting, 4, 6, 10, 13, 14, 16, 19
Northeast Canyons and Seamounts Marine National Monument, 26, 27

O
oil drilling, 21
oil spills, 21, 22
overfishing, 6, 21

P
population decline, 7, 22
predators, 14, 16
Project Puffin, 27
puffin hunting, 25

R
range, 6, 21, 22, 25
research, 7, 18, 19, 21, 27

S
starvation, 18, 19, 21

T
threats, 6, 7, 18, 19, 21, 22, 27

U
United States, 26

W
Westman Islands, 4, 6

3 1333 04783 1795